AF281540

How to Effectively Network Within Professional Organizations

dr. Franci Jezek

Copyright

First Edition

Production and publishing:
BoD – Books on Demand, Norderstedt
ISBN: 9783759751461

FSC
www.fsc.org

MIX
Papier aus verantwortungsvollen Quellen
Paper from responsible sources
FSC® C105338

Chapter 1: Join Wisely

The first step in effective networking within professional organizations is to choose the right organizations to join. Remember, it's not the speed that matters, it is the right direction you are headed to.

This chapter will guide you through the process of selecting organizations that align with your goals and offer the best opportunities for meaningful connections.

The Importance of Quality Over Quantity

When it comes to joining professional organizations, it's crucial to prioritize quality over quantity. It's far more beneficial to be an active member of a few well-chosen organizations than to spread yourself thin across many groups. Here's why:

1. Focus: Being part of fewer organizations allows you to dedicate more time and energy to each one, leading to deeper involvement and stronger connections. If possible, chose only one or maybe two. Focusing down will let your resources be more actively involved in the right areas and you will reap the most benefits.

2. Relevance: By carefully selecting organizations, you ensure that your time is spent in environments directly relevant to your career goals and interests. Usually, the more general organizations are not advised, unless you are looking for new sales. If you are looking for gaining expertise and recognition, use environment that are niched, specific to your situation. Remember it is better to create one and be the founder than be a no one in a million member society.

3. Reputation: Active participation in respected organizations can enhance your professional reputation more effectively than superficial involvement in numerous groups. Think about it this way. What would you like to see on a prospective new employee, a dozen od different memberships, or one exclusive one. Settling on one,

means you are focused on, settling on a lot, means you are still finding directions. Which one do you want to be?

4. Return on Investment: Your time and often money are valuable resources. Focusing on quality organizations ensures a better return on your investment in terms of networking opportunities and professional growth. Any society that is meaningful to enter has a fee. And a lot of activities you need to be a part of. It is just how they filter out the interested from the rest. So use your resources wisely. That being said, do not try to mistake price entry for quality – it can be an indicator for a hypothesis to test out, but it sure isn't proof.

Aligning with Career Goals

Selecting organizations that align with your career goals is crucial for effective networking. Consider the following:

1. Industry Relevance: Choose organizations specific to your industry or field of expertise. Niching is better than generalization. You probably want to be an expert in the field of X, not a jack of all trades.

2. Career Stage: Look for groups that cater to professionals at your career level or the level you aspire to reach. It is better to be a member of a level up or same level, than staying at the beginner level. Of course that doesn't mean you can't be a contributor to society of younger versions of yourself. It just means, that your growth focus should be somewhere else – higher.

3. Skill Development: Seek organizations that offer opportunities to develop skills you want to enhance. Define what skills you can and want to improve. Research what skill development can be of use to you, even if you don't find it valuable (yet). Speaking publicly can seem a waste of time for a technical job, but if you grow through the rank, you will need to learn to do it sooner rather than later.

4. Geographic Scope: Decide whether local, national, or international organizations best suit your career ambitions. A healthy dose of local and international connection is usually the best recipe. I would

suggest the pareto principle – 80/20, depending on where your potential lies. If your customers are international, lean more on international, if local, lean more on local. But do not forget the other side – things can change quickly, and you want to get a pulse on local/international trends before they run you over.

How to Choose the Right Organization

Follow these steps to identify and select the most suitable professional organizations:

1. Define Your Objectives: Clearly articulate what you hope to gain from joining a professional organization. This could include networking opportunities, continuing education, industry insights, or leadership experience. It is a hard choice, but you should have the data before you decide which ones (from the top 5) you personally like. Objectives are long term, so you should probably like being a member with them too.

2. Research Thoroughly: Use online resources, professional journals, and recommendations from colleagues to create a list of potential organizations. Any informational resource is valuable to you. It is not just what others see in the organization, it is also what you feel about it. What works for one person may perhaps not work for you.

3. Evaluate Benefits: Look closely at what each organization offers. Consider factors such as:
   - Networking events and opportunities
   - Professional development resources
   - Industry recognition or certifications
   - Access to job boards or career services
   - Mentorship programs

4. Assess the Membership: Look into the current membership of the organization. Are there professionals you admire or would like to connect with? Is there a good mix of experience levels? Will it serve your networking and professional needs for the next few years?

5. Consider the Commitment: Understand the time and financial commitments required. This includes membership fees, time for meetings or events, and any volunteer expectations. Consider opportunity cost of not doing something else while being active and engaged in the network. Consider sometimes getting early or staying late, how that will change your daily life and routine.

6. Try Before You Buy: Many organizations allow guests to attend meetings or events. Take advantage of these opportunities to get a feel for the organization before committing. Also, sometimes they have a newbie program, that gets you appointed a mentor, a lower fee and a lot of materials for you to catch up. Inquire if your network has such a thing, don't be coy. Sometimes they won't have it, but they will make something just for you.

7. Read Reviews and Testimonials: Look for feedback from current or past members to get an idea of their experiences. Be carefull who you listen to, you need to find a testimonial or review from somebody who has a similar experience, background and experience. If you can't find any, try to get as much information from different types of peers as possible.

Maximizing Your Membership

Once you've joined an organization, make the most of your membership with these strategies:

1. Attend Events Regularly: Consistency is key in building relationships. Make an effort to attend as many events as possible. Just by showing up, you are building relationships and a brand of yourself. And you do want to be remembered as somebody who is reliable and "just shows up when promised".

2. Volunteer: Offer to help with event planning, join a committee, or take on a leadership role. This increases your visibility and demonstrates your commitment. An hour a month can go a long way, when others drag their feet to make a commitment of 2 hours per year. See what the standard is and try to surpass it by 20%.

3. Utilize Resources: Take full advantage of the organization's offerings, such as webinars, workshops, or online forums. Read up as much as you can. If you find something outdated, suggest to get it up to date and send it for approval to somebody important. You will gain bonus points and an access level to someone in charge. As the romans said - Quid pro quo. You give to receive bonus points.

4. Network Strategically: Don't just connect with people in your immediate circle. Seek out diverse connections across different roles and experience levels. Strategically doesn't mean go for the higher guns immediately, build some base first with other people. You will gain some inside information and won't be seen as a cliché of a newbie.

5. Share Your Expertise: Offer to speak at events or contribute to the organization's publications. This positions you as an expert in your field. If you have something to share, offer to share, via articles, webinars or presentations. Also, make sure to make that opportunities available to you to share – keep in mind that you may have an edge on something, so use it to gain an edge in something else. Like a young new member will probably be better in AI and software than a more experienced member.

6. Stay Informed: Keep up with the organization's communications and industry news to stay relevant in conversations. Keep up with the organizational bulletins is one thing. Keeping up with the vibe of the industry is sometime more subtle. Knowing who is who in the industry can be a gamechanger. Especially, if you happen to connect with someone close to a "whale".

7. Seek Mentorship: If the organization offers a mentorship program, consider participating either as a mentee or mentor. Mentorship is a bit about an illusion of ego – either you boost your own, or you help boost somebody else's. If done correctly, the best networkers do both.

8. Provide Feedback: Share constructive feedback with the organization's leadership. This shows your engagement and can help improve the organization for all members. Be vary of critic, but be

gracious with praises and thank yours. A simple thank you email can distinguish yourself from the others. 5 minutes and your are somebody who they remember – for something that made them feel good.

By carefully selecting and fully engaging with the right professional organizations, you lay a strong foundation for effective networking. Remember, the goal is not just to join, but to become an active, valuable member of a community that aligns with your professional aspirations.

Chapter 2: Engage Actively

Once you've joined the right professional organizations, the next crucial step is to engage actively. You made the downpayment for joining the race, now you need to stack your deck to cash all in.

This chapter will guide you through effective strategies for participation and outline the benefits of being an involved member.

Strategies for Active Engagement

1. Regular Attendance
   Consistently attending meetings and events is the foundation of active engagement. It shows commitment and provides regular opportunities to connect with other members.

   - Set reminders for upcoming events. It helps if you have an accountability buddy or a mentor. Give them a reminder for coming – a simple you are coming is fine. Or "did you see that point on the schedule"?
   - Block out time in your calendar for organization activities. Remember that the real networking usually takes place before and after the formal event. Be there and shake some hands.
   - If you can't attend in person, look for virtual participation options. Write some DMs, connect to them on LinkedIn with a note saying that you saw them on the list.

2. Participate in Discussions
   Don't be a passive observer. Contribute to conversations, both during formal sessions and informal networking times.

   - Prepare questions in advance for speakers or panelists. Don't be to pesky. If it is a difficult or in depth question, try to have them delivered beforehand. Nobody want's to be ambushed with questions like on a pop up quiz.
   - Share your experiences or insights when relevant. It will feel awkward at first, but practice makes it more tolerable.

- Practice active listening to engage meaningfully in discussions. Most people welcome an insight and a question, because involvement means you care about the subject that they care.

3. Volunteer for Roles and Responsibilities

Taking on responsibilities within the organization increases your visibility and demonstrates your commitment.

- Join a committee or task force. Propose to form one and give suggestion on what, how and who.
- Offer to help organize events. A pair of hands is always helpful at events. Even just to be standby to step in in case of absence.
- Volunteer to lead a project or initiative. But don't be too pushy, suggest to be a member and mention you would be willing to help if needed.

4. Share Your Expertise

Find opportunities to showcase your knowledge and skills. Not everyone has the same skills. So try sharing your skills with those who haven't got them.

- Offer to give a presentation on your area of expertise. Or a short summary of it. Or a contribution in industry bulletin.
- Write articles for the organization's newsletter or blog. Share it with others on the media.
- Mentor newer members in your field. Show your commitment to the cause of the network itself.

5. Network Intentionally

Make a conscious effort to meet new people at each event. If you added a 100 people to your connection list each week you would be living just on that. The more people you know, the easier it gets. You either get a referral, introduction, or you know what somebody is into, by asking someone else.

- Set a goal to introduce yourself to a certain number of new people per month, week, day.

- Follow up with new contacts after the event. A quick recap of what you talked about does wonders. It shows you remembered them and makes them feel special.

- Look for ways to connect people with similar interests or complementary skills. You have an easy way into that one – you already share the same things to get your conversation started.

Effective Engagement Techniques

1. Be Prepared

- Research speakers or topics before events. Asking smart questions can raise some eyebrows. Be humble enough not to be seen as attacking, but show you have done your homework.

- Prepare an elevator pitch about yourself and your work. A well knitted introduction, research and a pitch can leave a lasting impression.

- Bring business cards or have a digital alternative ready. While business cards can be slowly going extinct, try to find ways for the person to take something from you with which they will remember you by. A pocket can opener/screwdriver is something that men usually like very well and it can cost as little as a few cents, when ordered in bulk. A nice working (do not buy cheap ones, that will break – you don't want to be associated with that one – that is why I always avoid umbrellas as tokens) pen or pencil is also a great reminder.

2. Show Genuine Interest in Others

- Ask open-ended questions about others' work and interests. Be curious about them. Listen and ask some more. See where they spark up.

- Remember details about people you meet and reference them in future interactions. That will help you remember them and it will make them feel good. "How's that beekeeping doing" will make wonders.

- Look for ways to help or support other members. If you can help, do it. Think of it in the long-term or as carma.

3. Contribute to Online Platforms

- Participate in the organization's online forums or social media groups. You write it once and it stays there for years to come. So don't write something silly. Make some effort into it. Unless it is a good way to implement an innocent joke.

- Share relevant industry news or insights. Being a curator saves time to others. Leaving a link for others to catch up is also great.

- Engage with and comment on others' posts. Don't do it for just the comment sake. If you can't write something to add value or meaningful, don't do it.

4. Seek and Offer Feedback

- Ask for input on your ideas or projects. It is a fair way to test out your ideas or project. People in your network will more likely give you some feedback. Perhaps it will not be usefull, but at least you are getting some feedback. Too often you are constrained how to get good reviews at the start. By reciving some from your network, you will usually have a greater chance of getting feedback, although it will usually be a bit more positive or washed down.

- Provide constructive feedback when asked. When somebody asks for feedback, try to give genuine feedback and advice. You want to be a go-to guy/girl for feedback, because that will bring you so much new possibilities and opportunities. Be positive, remember it is hard to ask for feedback on your project and people will identify personally with the project itself, try not to hurt their feelings and give valuable feedback as well.

- Be open to criticism and use it as an opportunity for growth. It is hard to listen to something critical. But bear in mind that it probably hurts, because you know it is at least partly true. Try to listen as carefully as possible, try to get to the bottom of it, ask detailed questions to extract all the possible value from that critic.

5. Balance Listening and Speaking

- Practice active listening to truly understand others' perspectives. You don't understand other people perspective until you can explain it even better than them. So explaining it back to them like they had no clue about it and they were 9 years old. If they will correct you, excellent, you are building rapport, redo the repeating/rewording now. A good communicator is always hard to find – you will feel astounded how many opportunities will open up to you by just listening and paraphrasing.

- Share your own thoughts and experiences but avoid dominating conversations. You have two ears and one mouth, so you should listen twice as much as you speak. Do not dominate the conversation. Especially, if the other person is passionate about a subject, you should listen carefully – extract all the information about the subject and about the person, that you can.

- Look for opportunities to build on others' ideas. By giving a positive, constructive suggestion how to improve or even build of another person's idea, you become an invaluable partner they just can't and won't ignore. You just opened the door for yourself, now build on that opportunity.

Overcoming Barriers to Participation

1. Time Constraints

- Prioritize events that align most closely with your goals. Sometimes you cannot attend the event, either logistically, financially or for some other reason. That is fine. Your time is your precious resource. And while for networking it is best to attend as much of events as possible, you will still reach a point when you have to decide which one to attend and which not. That is why setting clear goals for your journey at the network is crucial. Attend those events that align with your long-term goal at the network. You need to grow first, everything else is only food, water and building blocks to achieve that goal.

- Look for ways to integrate organization activities into your work or personal development time. Sometimes you must work hard to attend an event. Other times you can kill two flies with one swing. While using a personal or work time can de-focus your networking time, it is still much better than not to attend at all, or to do it and it being difficult or with a lot of friction. Frictionless activities are best to be used as much as possible.

- Consider virtual participation options for events you can't attend in person. Sometimes virtual event is the least worst option. Use it to network virtually and try to be seen by posing questions or sending them beforehand. Your networking efficiency might as well not be as good as in person, but you can still achieve many things.

2. Shyness or Introversion

- Start small by setting achievable engagement goals. Big groups can be intimidating, especially if you are entering a group where members already know each other. Use it to your advantage – you will gain curiosity in at least some members. Address them first. Even a simple hello, where does the next venue take place, is a great conversational starter. Or simple be humble and tell straight up – I do not know anybody, it is quite frustrating. Wished I knew who is who here. Most often than not, the other party will give you some information and you will bond. And if everything else fails, try to find another new member and mingle with him. At least you got one more node in your network, right. And because you both are in a tough spor, the connection might as well be tighter than a loose one.

- Prepare conversation starters in advance. Sometimes you will know who you meet and where/why. It is good to have some conversation starters by hand. A good salesman taught me that – he simply googled some people that he thought might be there. And if they were (most often at least one, if not more), he would have a great conversation starter at hand and a rapport to build easily. A couple minutes of homework, a couple years of sales connection worth tens of thousands.

- Partner with a more outgoing colleague or friend for support at events. If you are really scared/anxious about the event, grab a talker and go with him/her. It will ease the anxiety and you will still be able to grab some of the connections with him. Better a network node by proxy than no node at all.

3. Imposter Syndrome

- Remember that everyone has unique experiences and insights to share. Remember everybody gets imposter syndrome from time to time. Not everybody likes to talk about it. Remember you have something to offer for this world, or you would not even know about this network or opportunity. No matter the level, you have something to offer. Usually the people most plagued by imposter syndrome have the most to offer.

- Focus on learning and growth rather than comparison. It is hard to objectively compare, so it is wise not to do it at all. The problem is that you are probably comparing yourself to a perception of another person, not the real person. While being a cliché (but also true), you should really compare yourself today to where you were a month, a year, a decade ago. Everything else is just false data comparison.

- Celebrate your successes and contributions, no matter how small they may seem. There seems to be two directions people go – either they praise meaningless achievement, or they shy away from celebrating big wins. If those would be the only options, go for the praise of everything. Your brain and ego needs some praise boost. Let that dopamine flow and improve your mood to open up to seek new opportunities.

4. Lack of Immediate Results
- Understand that building a network takes time. Frequency will always beat intensity. A short-term goal can be achieved in 90 days, so do not expect no overnight success. A gravitational network that will change lives takes years to build and nurture, before it can be harvested for its benefits. That being said, do not shy away from a chance of luck if it falls into your lap. But do not seek it or expect it.

- Set realistic expectations for the outcomes of your engagement. It is wise to make time plans for your goals and add some buffer to it. Beating your own numbers can sound rewarding, but everything meaningfull takes time. Lots of time. Time for stuff you did not even plan, because you did not know it existed, that you had to do it, or because you assumed it would not break and you would need to fix it. I read a story from Rick Voss (never split the difference) where the team that approached the problem the fastest, took on average 2 days to a solution, the team that took the longest to approach, took an average of 6 hours to a solution. A solution meaning saving lives. So why would you rush into something, if you knew that this speed can get you killed or lose a deal or connection. Take your time and do the small talk and check the pulse of the environment.

- Keep track of small wins and progress to stay motivated. A wall of fame or a wall of success is a good reminder where you came from and where you are going. It also keeps the imposter syndrome and the comparison fail at bay.

5. Difficulty Balancing Multiple Commitments
- Be selective about which activities you commit to. Remember cherry pick the long-term activities first. Then add some more.
- Communicate clearly about your availability and limitations. Neither you, or your partner or your network want you somewhere all cranky. Either say yes, or say no. An honest yea is worth more than ghosting. Remember you want to be the person they can rely on – but that doesn't mean that you say yes to anything. It means if you say yes, you mean yes 100%.
- Look for ways to align organization activities with your other professional or personal goals. If luck or life gives you a pass to do two things at once, do not skip that opportunity.

Benefits of Active Engagement

1. Enhanced Professional Visibility
Active participation raises your profile within your industry or field. Write articles, posts, ask questions, volunteer. The bar for being seen is usually very low – people just don't seem to care or want to do the extra 1%.

2. Expanded Network
Regular engagement leads to more diverse and meaningful professional connections. You want to establish a bran of good will. You need to be known for something positive and your reputation will expand out of the formal network.

3. Skill Development
Involvement in various activities can help you develop new skills or refine existing ones. Sometimes you can improve skills in your field. Sometimes you improve skills you do not (yet) need. Be open to learning and new ideas – they may be valuable in more ways than one.

4. Access to Opportunities
Active members often learn about job openings, collaborations, or other opportunities before they're widely known. Being well

connected means also you are well informed. You can also refer a person for an opening and gain two benefits (the employee and the employer) – just do not refer somebody you will feel a headache later.

5. Personal Growth

Stepping out of your comfort zone to engage actively can boost confidence and interpersonal skills. You only grow by testing your limits and your shortcomings.

6. Industry Insights

Regular participation keeps you informed about the latest trends, challenges, and innovations in your field. You want to be as much ahead of the new trends as possible. Perhaps even start a trend or an innovation if possible. Then new innovation will first come to you for a feedback.

7. Leadership Experience

Taking on roles within the organization can provide valuable leadership experience. Nothing better than to test yourself as a leader in a low stakes role where the only input you had was to raise a hand when they needed a volunteer.

8. Sense of Community

Active engagement fosters a sense of belonging and support within your professional community. People like herd and a sense of belonging, use that to your advantage and foster the feeling.

Remember, the key to successful networking within professional organizations is consistent, genuine engagement.

By actively participating, you not only benefit personally and professionally but also contribute to the vitality and value of the organization as a whole.

Start small if needed, but commit to increasing your engagement over time.

The relationships and opportunities that result from your active involvement can be transformative for your career.

Chapter 3: Build Relationships

At the heart of effective networking lies the ability to build genuine, lasting relationships. This chapter will guide you through the art of creating meaningful connections within your professional organizations.

The Art of Genuine Connections

Building authentic relationships is more than exchanging business cards or adding contacts on LinkedIn. It's about creating mutual understanding, trust, and value. Here's how to approach relationship-building with authenticity:

1. Be Genuinely Interested
  - Show sincere curiosity about others' work, experiences, and perspectives. If you feel interested, people will tell you stuff. Sometimes wild, sometimes useful. But you will have an abundance of information.
  - Ask thoughtful questions that go beyond surface-level small talk. Asking questions is the second level of listening. Use it.
  - Practice active listening, giving your full attention to the person you're speaking with. Ask question by repeating to them, and asking to confirm, you understood correctly.

2. Be Yourself
  - Don't try to be someone you're not – authenticity is key to building trust. You can't fake it in the long run, and people will sense you are trying to be someone you are not. Try to be as authentic as possible, while being civilized and positive.
  - Share your own experiences and insights honestly. The best stories involve failure and mistakes. With a sense of humor.
  - Be open about your goals and challenges, if you feel like it. Some like to share goals, some like to ponder on them. Sharing goals is usually good to keep you accountable. But hiding them gives you a better place to rethink them. If a detailed goal means a lot to you, you should probably share it, as people will see you light up speaking about it and they will naturally try to help you achieve it.

3. Focus on Quality Over Quantity
- Aim for meaningful conversations rather than trying to meet everyone in the room. Hopping from a person to person is a horrible habbit and a way someone from the past thought how networking is done. It is really done by talking to 1-3 people per event.
- Take the time to get to know people beyond their job titles. The deeper the connection, the longer it will last and the bigger the value. The initial build-up and impression will probably last longer than you think.
- Follow up with those you connect with to deepen the relationship. A simple email, a connection request, even an Instagram dm of a reel will do so much to add value to a connection.

4. Offer Value First
- Look for ways to help others without expecting immediate returns. It is best to give first and not have an immediate ask. That will make the person you are connecting trust you more and provide a more meaningful connection.
- Share relevant information, resources, or connections that might benefit your new contacts. Sometimes connecting two of your dots together is the way you become more connected.
- Be generous with your time and knowledge. Remember you are not here to reap the rewards tomorrow, but to grow value for the future.

Strategies for Building Lasting Professional Relationships

1. Find Common Ground
- Look for shared interests, experiences, or challenges. People like people who like similar things. Either by doing some homework, or by listening carefully and some probing, try to find a common ground with the person you are trying to connect to.
- Use these commonalities as a foundation for building rapport. Once you have established some common ground, it is so much easier to build that relationship. It greases the ease of making that

foundation. The more specific the common ground is, the more likely it will last more.

2. Be Consistent and Reliable
- Follow through on promises or commitments you make. Nobody wants to befriend people who do not honor what they say. They are a joke and an unreliable joke to top off that. Follow through or say no beforehand.
- Maintain regular contact, not just when you need something. Put a reminder in your calendar to drop a message or a short phone call at least once every quarter. Make it a bit random, so it isn't on the same day every 3 months, but make it a schedule. You need to invest in a relationship in order for it to be viable or to grow.

3. Show Appreciation
- Express gratitude for others' time, insights, or help. A simple thank you note for being my friend once a year, perhaps even combined with a b-day card does a long way. It is nice, personal and it makes you both feel positive about the relationship. And the other person will probably reciprocate and make you feel better.
- Recognize and celebrate others' achievements. Cheers their winds and they will root for yours. Be their when they are down, but most importantly, celebrate with them, when they are on the pedestal of winners.

4. Be Patient
- Understand that strong relationships take time to develop. Relationships are like trees – they need to be planted, then nurtured for a long time till you can have something from them, like a shade, a fruit, or both.
- Don't rush or force connections – let them evolve naturally. It's kind of a power law – the more you force it, the harder it is. Make sure all the beneficial factors of a growing relationship environment exist, but do not force it. Let is grow it's natural course.

5. Practice Empathy
- Try to understand others' perspectives and challenges. Each person has this three levels of life – the public one, the private one and the secret one. If you manage to get into the secret one, you are "IN". In

order to do that, you need either a lot of time & effort, or a good understanding of what the persons perspective, postions and challenges are.

- Offer support during difficult times. A simple "I am here, if you need me" can mean a lot. Or a simple ear to listen to a problem in life, without judging.

6. Maintain Professional Boundaries

- While friendliness is important, remember to keep relationships professional. Do not try to blur the professional/friendship line, unless both of you really want to. Sometimes maintaining a profesionall and friendship relationship can be tricky and difficult because professional goals can contradict friendship goals. While not being impossible, it can put a strain onto relationship you don't need. Some even suggest not crossing the line at all costs. I would argue there are all flavours in life and you cannot predict what life will bring. Some even network and then marry. So who am I to tell you something absolute. Except to be cautios, because when things go wrong, they go wrong professionals and in the friendship zone.

- Be respectful of others' time and personal space. You will find clues how someone values their time and personal space. Do not try to cross that line – you will seem to pushy and the other person will resent you. Too often I put people on the block list just because they are too pushy in getting what they want immediately. And I know I am not alone.

Nurturing Your Network

Building relationships is an ongoing process. Here are strategies to maintain and strengthen your professional connections over time:

1. Regular Check-ins

- Schedule periodic catch-ups with key contacts. Make it intentional, but do not come across as deliberate. You want to at least make an appearance of a random catch-up, not a deliberate stalk-in.

- Use various communication channels (email, phone, in-person meetings) based on the relationship and circumstances. The more variety of communication you use, the less likely you will be seen as too utilitarian (see Machiavelli on that one - ☺).

2. Share Relevant Information
- Forward articles, reports, or news that might interest your contacts. A curator of knowledge is useful to have around. And people will share new (perhaps even unpublished) information to you beforehand in order to feed your curator role. Remember to thank them in some way – either in person, or giving credit (check if they want it or want to remain anonymous) or by giving some favors.
- Keep them informed about developments in your shared field of interest. Sometimes it is hard to keep track of all the progress in different bringe fields. If something might be usefull, keep them in the loop. Perhaps even drop a line why you think it would be usefull to them, although it does not seem that way at first glance.

3. Offer Ongoing Support
- Be available when your contacts need advice or assistance. Be the helping hand you want others to be to you.
- Offer to make introductions or provide references when appropriate. If you see a mutual benefit between two nodes of network, if you connect them together do it. If it turns out good, they will be very gratefull. Usually people are grateful even if it does not turn out perfect, just because you thought about their interests.

4. Attend Industry Events Together
- Invite contacts to accompany you to relevant conferences or seminars. Drop an email you will be going and why. Perhaps they would gladly join, if they knew that somebody they know will also be attending.
- Use these shared experiences as opportunities to deepen your connection. As you create new stories, these new events bind you together even further.

5. Collaborate on Projects
- Look for opportunities to work together on professional initiatives. If possible, collaborate. Nothing better than knowing someone on the other side, because you have already established trust.

- Propose joint presentations or co-authoring articles. Splitting the credit is a must. Push them to develop those skills or give credit, it will make an impression of a giver. And then you can later make the big ask, if you need to.

6. Celebrate Successes

- Acknowledge and congratulate your contacts on their achievements. Be happy that they achieved something. They will be happy for your wins also.
- Share in their joy and offer support during challenges. Be there to celebrate with them or offer a shoulder or an ear during the hard times.

7. Be a Resource

- Position yourself as a go-to person for information or advice in your area of expertise. Usually adding just 1% effort than the average can make you become a go-to person. With a little bit of luck and a persistence you will the go-to person.
- Be willing to connect others in your network when it's mutually beneficial. Give back and be humble.

8. Seek Feedback

- Ask for honest input on your ideas or work. Ask for feedback even if you are sure in what you are doing. A second perspective is always useful. Also, it establishes a safe environment to give and receive feedback when you actually must have it.
- Show appreciation for constructive criticism and use it to improve. Don't just ask for it, act upon it and provide feedback on using the feedback to improve. Sometimes it won't be useful, but that's ok. Tell them you tried another direction, although you kept their feedback in mind.

Overcoming Challenges in Relationship Building

1. Limited Time

- Prioritize relationships that align most closely with your professional goals. All resources are scarce. But time is the most scarce resource of them all.

- Use technology to stay connected (e.g., scheduling tools, video calls). It can give you an edge to leverage more activities than if you just did them in person.
- Combine relationship-building with other professional activities. Try out different things, make it fun for you and your network.

2. Geographic Distance
- Leverage virtual communication tools for regular check-ins. Sometimes the distance is so big, there is no other option than virtual. Make it count.
- Make the most of in-person opportunities when they arise. When you do meet, use every second of it intentionally, if possible. Prepare.
- Engage actively in online professional communities. Because online impressions are more shallow, you need to reinforce them more frequently.

3. Diverse Personalities
- Adapt your communication style to suit different individuals. The best communicators mimic the style of their counterparts. You would do well to heed this advice.
- Find common ground even with those who seem very different from you. You can find common ground with almost everybody, if you are willing and persistent enough.
- Practice patience and open-mindedness. Be patient, resilient (not pushy), and open-minded, that any person can teach you something.

4. Maintaining Multiple Relationships
- Use a customer relationship management (CRM) tool to track interactions. Either a professional one (like for sales) or a personal one (some people suggest this app Dex, that links up to LinkedIn). It will help with the reach-outs and keeping up frequent check-ins.
- Set reminders for follow-ups and check-ins. Use old-school planner or software to remind you.
- Prioritize depth of relationships over sheer numbers. If you have to choose, choose quality over quantity. Better shed that 10% of contact and improve 10% of frequency with the other.

5. Dealing with Conflict

- Address misunderstandings or disagreements promptly and professionally. Always assume the best intentions and you will have them less. Always tell them you had the best intentions and what they were as soon as possible, to stop their negativity bias into building a fake story. If something can be interpreted ambiguous, start by saying you have a positive stance and how. Follow up with asking if they understood the good intention and the essence of the story and motives.

- Seek to understand the other person's perspective. If you can look at the situation from other person's perspective, you will usually avoid most land-mines in the relationship.

- Focus on finding mutually beneficial solutions. Say it, mean it and act upon it.

The Long-Term Benefits of Strong Professional Relationships

1. Career Opportunities

- Access to job openings, promotions, or new projects. If you are well connected, you will be offered jobs before they are even published or actively looking. Promotions will happen, because they will be scared of loosing you. New projects will be on your table, so you will have to say no more often than yes.

- Recommendations and referrals from trusted contacts. You will be recommended and referred by people who matter. You will already have a foot in the door, so to speak, even before you actively know what it is about.

2. Knowledge Exchange

- Insights into industry trends and best practices. You will gain insights into trends well before others do. You will be there to either get acquainted or to even form best practices adopted in your industry.

- Exposure to diverse perspectives and experiences. You will be exposed to new ideas and start to think about things more creatively.

3. Professional Support

- A network of advisors and mentors to guide your career decisions. A well connected person can pick up a phone to get advice or a mentor on a subject. Because the person on the other side knows they will be good on it when the time comes.

- Emotional support during professional challenges. Sometimes a simple "yes it's hard" from a peer is all you need to get through.

4. Increased Influence

- Greater ability to effect change within your industry or organization. You are in the midst of the action, and it is up to you to make it go into a direction you think is best. If you do the work.

- Enhanced professional reputation through association with respected peers. Peers lift each other up, especially networked peers.

5. Personal Growth

- Opportunities to develop new skills and broaden your horizons. Growth capabilities will be everywhere if you will be open to look and act upon it.

- Increased self-awareness through interactions with diverse professionals. Your luck will increase because you will have the experts' eye on lucky opportunity now. Not the lame, beginner one, but the expert one.

6. Business Development

- Potential for new clients, partnerships, or collaborations. New connections mean new people to sell to, to partner with or to ask for a collaboration.

- Access to a wider range of resources and expertise. You are now in a group that takes care of each own, you have therefore access to a wider range of resources. Provided you give something back, you can become a force to reckon with.

Remember, building strong professional relationships is a long-term investment in your career. It requires patience, authenticity, and a genuine desire to contribute to others' success. By focusing on creating meaningful connections and nurturing them over time, you'll develop a robust network that can support and enhance your professional journey for years to come.

Chapter 4: Follow Up

One of the most critical yet often overlooked aspects of networking is the follow-up. This chapter will explore why following up is crucial and how to do it effectively to strengthen your professional relationships.

The Crucial Step of Following Up

Following up after initial meetings or interactions is what transforms a brief encounter into a lasting connection. Here's why it's so important:

1. Reinforces the Connection: It reminds the person of your interaction and keeps you fresh in their mind. Think of it this way, they have a forgetting factor of 80%, and by following up, you increase it for 25%, so you don't loose, but gain a bit. With every follow up.

2. Shows Professionalism: Following up demonstrates that you're organized, reliable, and value the relationship. By following up you know and they know, that you are not led by inspiration but by a goal and perseverance to establish a plan to that goal.

3. Opens Doors for Further Interaction: It provides an opportunity to continue the conversation and deepen the connection. Every interaction is also an opportunity to get something deeper or something new.

4. Helps You Stand Out: In a world where many neglect to follow up, doing so can set you apart. By paying attention to catching up or remembering important dates you have already surpassed the bar of average.

5. Builds Trust: Consistent follow-ups over time help establish trust and credibility. Being reliable to reach out and catch up, means also, you will honor your promises and commitments.

Effective Follow-Up Strategies

1. Timing is Everything
   - Follow up within 24-48 hours of the initial meeting. Got to feed that impression while it is still fresh, in order for it to grow.
   - For events, follow up with new contacts within a week. It make some time to get into the natural flow of life, so a little more time might be wise.
   - Set reminders if needed to ensure timely follow-ups. Use a reminder software or a simple google calendar to set up an alert. You do not want to forget.

2. Personalize Your Message
   - Reference specific details from your conversation. Do not send generic unpersonal messages.
   - Mention any shared interests or experiences. This will make them remember more and build better relationships.
   - Avoid generic or templated messages. They should be avoided at all costs. Better to not send anything at all than make an unpersonal message ruin the connection for good.

3. Choose the Right Medium
   - Email is often appropriate for initial follow-ups. It can be informal, can be formal. Always be on the positive side.
   - LinkedIn can be suitable for professional contexts. Request a connection, but always send a note with it. Do not leave it blank. Requests with a side note have such a higher percentage of likelihood to succeed.
   - Consider the person's preferred communication method if known. If somebody really hates social media and told you so, send a letter or an email to them. Meet them half way in their world so to speak.

4. Be Clear and Concise
   - Keep your message brief and to the point. They are probably busy, as we are all. Make it formal, upbeat, but short and to the point.
   - Clearly state the purpose of your follow-up. So often a concise why is missing and the reader wondering about it. You want to express it clearly.

- End with a specific call to action or next step. What do you want. They know you want something, so you should not hide it. Be polite, clear and concise in your ask. Also try to eliminate all the friction preventing them to help you (like asking for additional information that can be already provided in your ask/email).

5. Provide Value
 - Share a relevant article, resource, or introduction. Contribute to their growth and they will see to that you grow as well.
 - Offer assistance or information related to your conversation. Offer a video call or a help-out session if you can.
 - Follow through on any promises made during your initial interaction. Deliver and exceed any expectations. It is usually easy, as people are usually not full of trust to begin with. Surprise them.

6. Be Authentic
 - Express genuine interest in continuing the relationship. Do not fake it, adopt the mentality itself. Being curious and sociably likeable can be a huge asset.
 - Share something about yourself to foster a two-way connection. Do not leave it just professional or share a funny work anecdotes. Remember not to put any third person on the spot. Rather focus on the situation itself.
 - Avoid overly formal language; aim for a professional yet friendly tone. Positivity over critical negativeness. We all have enough negativity already present in our everyday life.

7. Suggest Next Steps
 - Propose a specific action, such as a coffee meeting or phone call. Be proactive in how to move things along.
 - Offer multiple options to accommodate their schedule. Try using a scheduling app or offer at least 3 alternatives.
 - Be clear about your intentions for further interaction. Make sure what they will get from it and you will.

Sample Follow-Up Messages

1. After a Conference:

"Hello [Name],

It was great meeting you at [Conference Name] yesterday. I enjoyed our conversation about [specific topic]. I thought you might find this article on [related subject] interesting: [link]. Would you be open to continuing our discussion over coffee next week? I'd love to hear more about your work on [their project/interest].

Best regards,

[Your Name]"

2. After a Job Interview:

"Dear [Interviewer's Name],

Thank you for taking the time to meet with me yesterday regarding the [Position] role. Our conversation about [specific topic discussed] further increased my enthusiasm for the position and the company. I'm excited about the possibility of bringing my skills in [relevant skill] to your team. Please don't hesitate to contact me if you need any additional information.

I look forward to hearing from you about the next steps in the process.

Sincerely,

[Your Name]"

3. After a Networking Event:

"Hi [Name],

It was a pleasure meeting you at [Event Name] last night. I was impressed by your insights on [topic discussed]. As promised, I'm sending you the link to that [resource/article] we talked about: [link]. I'd be interested in hearing your thoughts on it.

Would you be interested in grabbing coffee sometime next week to continue our conversation? I'd love to learn more about your experience with [their area of expertise].

Best,

[Your Name]"

Timing and Frequency of Follow-Ups

1. Initial Follow-Up

- Send within 24-48 hours of the first meeting. Impression is still fresh, so up it with a follow up.
- Keep it brief and reference your conversation. Quick and dirty. Or quick and efficient rather than long and unamusing.

2. Second Follow-Up
- If you don't receive a response, wait about a week before following up again. People can be busy at the time, so waiting a week is giving them air to breathe.
- Reiterate your interest in connecting and offer a specific reason or benefit. Better yet both – a gain for them and an interest for you.

3. Ongoing Communication
- After establishing initial contact, maintain the relationship with periodic check-ins. Preferably quarterly, unless industry specific otherwise.
- The frequency can vary based on the nature of the relationship, but aim for at least quarterly contact. Use different media over the quarterly contact – email, calls, social media, physical cards/letters.

4. Event-Based Follow-Ups
- Reach out when you come across something relevant to their interests or work. Especially if you know they will like it.
- Congratulate them on achievements or milestones you become aware of. Do it publicly and also with a separate private message. If appropriate, send a gift basket.

5. Annual Check-Ins
- For less close contacts, an annual holiday greeting or new year message can maintain the connection. But if you are sneaky even that can be sent more than once per year. International observance days, birthday or remembrance day of a famous person, etc can be a plausible excuse to send a card.

6. Before Making a Request
- If you need to ask for a favor, ensure you've had recent positive interactions first. Delay the ask as much as possible, unless confronted with it. Some people like to know who and why are they dealing with first. Now all recipes work on all people, adapt.

- Don't only reach out when you need something. Make it a pleasant experience for them. Ask if you can help with something. Think hard about doing something even if they don't ask and deliver to them privately.

Common Follow-Up Mistakes to Avoid

1. Waiting Too Long: Delayed follow-ups can lead to forgotten connections. You don't want to evoke: "Who is this again" response.

2. Being Too Pushy: Respect boundaries and don't overwhelm with frequent messages. Make the messages pleasant, sometimes if possible a bit less formal.

3. Lack of Personalization: Generic messages can feel insincere and unmemorable. Write a handwritten thank you card.

4. Focusing Only on Your Needs: Always consider how you can provide value to the other person. Think hard and think of something like your life depended on it – because your relationship does.

5. Neglecting to Follow Through: If you promise to send information or make an introduction, do it promptly. Before the due date, so you won't forget. Have it written in a calendar.

6. Improper Tone: Maintain a professional tone, even if your interaction was casual. Be sure to adjust the tone to the situation. Written communication must be very positive, to be considered neutral – it is just the way we perceive things. If possible, make a video call, you will have a variety of non-verbal cues to adjust your tone and messaging.

7. Spelling and Grammar Errors: Proofread your messages to ensure they're polished and error-free. Use a spell checker. Especially triple check their names.

8. Not Having a Clear Purpose: Each follow-up should have a specific goal or reason. Even if it just to meet or follow up next time.

Leveraging Technology for Follow-Ups

1. Customer Relationship Management (CRM) Tools
   - Use tools (Hubspot, SalesForce, etc) to track interactions and set reminders. Use personal CRM system (Dex, etc) to track any dates that are important to them or to you or to both.

2. LinkedIn
   - Utilize LinkedIn's features to stay updated on your contacts' professional activities
   - Use the platform's messaging system for professional follow-ups

3. Email Management Tools
   - Use tools like Boomerang or Followup.cc to schedule emails and reminders

4. Calendar Apps
   - Set reminders in your calendar app for follow-ups and check-ins

5. Social Media Monitoring
   - Use tools to track mentions of your contacts or their companies for timely follow-ups

Remember, effective follow-up is an ongoing process that requires consistency and genuine interest. By mastering the art of follow-up, you'll be able to turn brief encounters into meaningful professional relationships that can benefit your career for years to come.

Chapter 5: Stay Visible

In the world of professional networking, staying visible is crucial for maintaining and growing your connections. This chapter will explore strategies to keep yourself top of mind within your professional organizations and network.

Maintaining Your Presence

1. Consistent Participation
   - Regularly attend events, both in-person and virtual
   - Engage in online forums and discussions
   - Volunteer for committees or projects

2. Share Your Expertise
   - Offer to speak at events or webinars
   - Write articles for the organization's newsletter or blog
   - Contribute to industry publications

3. Be Active on Social Media
   - Share relevant content on professional platforms like LinkedIn
   - Engage with others' posts through thoughtful comments
   - Use appropriate hashtags to increase visibility

4. Network Continuously
   - Don't limit networking to formal events
   - Look for opportunities to connect in everyday professional situations
   - Maintain regular contact with key connections

Strategies for Staying Top of Mind

1. Provide Value Consistently
   - Share useful information, insights, or resources with your network
   - Offer help or support without expecting immediate returns
   - Be a connector, introducing people who could benefit from knowing each other

2. Develop a Personal Brand
   - Identify your unique strengths and expertise
   - Consistently communicate your professional identity across all platforms
   - Align your online presence with your offline persona

3. Create and Share Content
   - Start a professional blog or podcast
   - Write articles on LinkedIn or Medium
   - Create short video content sharing your expertise

4. Engage in Thought Leadership
   - Participate in panel discussions or roundtables
   - Comment on industry trends and developments
   - Share your unique perspective on professional challenges

5. Leverage Technology
   - Use social media management tools to maintain a consistent presence
   - Set up Google Alerts for industry keywords to stay informed
   - Use email marketing tools for newsletters or updates to your network

6. Celebrate Others' Successes
   - Acknowledge and share your connections' achievements
   - Offer genuine congratulations and support
   - This not only keeps you visible but also strengthens relationships

7. Be Responsive
   - Reply promptly to messages and invitations
   - Engage actively in discussions, both online and offline
   - Show that you're accessible and interested in your network

8. Attend Industry Events
   - Be present at key conferences and seminars in your field
   - Participate actively by asking questions or contributing to discussions

- Use these events as opportunities to reconnect with existing contacts and make new ones

Balancing Visibility and Authenticity

While staying visible is important, it's crucial to maintain authenticity in your interactions. Here are some tips to strike the right balance:

1. Be Genuine in Your Interactions
   - Don't force connections or conversations
   - Share real experiences and insights, not just what you think others want to hear
   - Be open about your challenges as well as your successes

2. Quality Over Quantity
   - Focus on meaningful interactions rather than trying to be everywhere all the time
   - Prioritize engagements that align with your professional goals and values

3. Respect Others' Time and Space
   - Be mindful of how often you reach out or share content
   - Ensure your contributions add value and aren't just noise

4. Stay True to Your Values
   - Don't compromise your principles for the sake of visibility
   - Align your visible activities with your core professional beliefs

5. Be Consistent Across Platforms
   - Maintain a cohesive professional image across all channels
   - Ensure your online presence reflects your real-world persona

6. Share Personal Insights Thoughtfully
   - While some personal sharing can make you more relatable, maintain professional boundaries
   - Focus on personal experiences that are relevant to your professional life

Overcoming Challenges in Maintaining Visibility

1. Time Constraints
   - Prioritize high-impact visibility activities
   - Use scheduling tools to maintain a consistent presence
   - Repurpose content across different platforms to maximize efficiency

2. Fear of Over-exposure
   - Focus on providing value rather than self-promotion
   - Vary your content and engagement methods to avoid repetition
   - Pay attention to feedback and adjust your approach accordingly

3. Introversion
   - Leverage written communication if you're more comfortable with it
   - Start with small, manageable visibility efforts and gradually increase
   - Find a visibility strategy that aligns with your personality

4. Changing Work Environments
   - Adapt your visibility strategies to new circumstances (e.g., remote work)
   - Look for innovative ways to stay connected in evolving professional landscapes
   - Be proactive in seeking out new visibility opportunities

5. Maintaining Relevance
   - Stay informed about industry trends and developments
   - Continuously update your skills and knowledge
   - Be open to feedback and willing to evolve your approach

The Long-Term Benefits of Staying Visible

1. Enhanced Professional Reputation
   - Consistent visibility helps establish you as a reliable and knowledgeable professional

2. Increased Opportunities
   - Being top of mind can lead to job offers, collaborations, or speaking engagements

3. Stronger Network
   - Regular engagement helps maintain and strengthen your professional relationships

4. Personal Brand Development
   - Consistent visibility contributes to a clear and recognizable personal brand

5. Industry Influence
   - Over time, visibility can lead to increased influence within your field

6. Continuous Learning
   - Staying visible often involves staying informed, leading to ongoing professional development

Remember, staying visible is not about constant self-promotion, but about consistently adding value to your professional community. By maintaining a thoughtful and authentic presence, you can build a strong professional reputation and create ongoing opportunities for growth and collaboration.

Chapter 6: Offer Value

One of the most effective ways to build and maintain a strong professional network is by consistently offering value to others. This chapter will explore the concept of value-based networking and provide strategies for becoming a valuable resource within your professional community.

The Power of Reciprocity in Networking

1. Understanding Reciprocity
   - Reciprocity is the social norm of responding to a positive action with another positive action
   - In networking, offering value creates a sense of obligation for others to reciprocate

2. Building Trust and Goodwill
   - Consistently offering value helps build trust and positive relationships
   - It positions you as a generous and supportive professional

3. Long-term Benefits
   - Value-based networking leads to more sustainable and mutually beneficial relationships
   - It creates a positive reputation that can open doors to future opportunities

Ways to Provide Value to Your Network

1. Share Knowledge and Expertise
   - Offer advice or insights in your area of expertise
   - Share relevant articles, research, or industry reports
   - Create and distribute original content (blog posts, whitepapers, podcasts)

2. Make Introductions
   - Connect people in your network who could benefit from knowing each other
   - Facilitate introductions thoughtfully, considering both parties' interests

3. Offer Mentorship
   - Guide less experienced professionals in your field
   - Share lessons from your own career journey

4. Provide Opportunities
   - Share job openings or project opportunities
   - Recommend qualified contacts for positions or collaborations

5. Give Thoughtful Feedback
   - Offer constructive feedback when asked
   - Provide testimonials or recommendations for colleagues' work

6. Volunteer Your Skills
   - Offer pro bono work for causes or organizations you support
   - Contribute your professional skills to community projects

7. Share Resources
   - Recommend useful tools or resources you've discovered
   - Offer templates, checklists, or other practical materials you've developed

8. Emotional Support
   - Be a good listener for colleagues facing professional challenges
   - Offer encouragement and motivation

9. Collaborate on Projects
   - Initiate or participate in collaborative efforts within your industry
   - Share credit and spotlight others' contributions

10. Recognize and Celebrate Others' Achievements
   - Publicly acknowledge the successes of others in your network
   - Share and promote others' accomplishments

Creating Win-Win Situations

1. Identify Mutual Benefits
   - Look for ways where offering value can also benefit you
   - Seek collaborations that leverage complementary skills

2. Align Value with Recipient's Needs
   - Understand the goals and challenges of your contacts
   - Tailor your offerings to address their specific situations

3. Be Strategic in Your Generosity
   - Focus on providing high-impact value rather than frequent, low-value interactions
   - Prioritize offering value to key relationships and those with potential for mutual growth

4. Create Opportunities for Reciprocation
   - When offering value, subtly indicate areas where you might benefit from their expertise
   - Be open about your own goals and challenges

5. Foster a Culture of Giving
   - Encourage others in your network to also offer value
   - Create a positive cycle of mutual support and generosity

Strategies for Consistently Offering Value

1. Stay Informed
   - Keep up-to-date with industry trends and developments
   - Continuously expand your knowledge and skills

2. Be Observant
   - Pay attention to the needs and interests of your network
   - Look for opportunities to offer timely and relevant value

3. Be Proactive
   - Don't wait to be asked; offer help when you see an opportunity
   - Reach out regularly with valuable insights or resources

4. Follow Through
   - If you offer to help, make sure to deliver on your promises
   - Be reliable and consistent in your value offerings

5. Personalize Your Approach
   - Tailor your value offerings to the individual's specific situation
   - Consider the recipient's communication preferences and professional context

6. Balance Giving and Receiving
   - While focusing on offering value, also be open to receiving help
   - Create a two-way flow of support and resources

7. Measure and Adjust
   - Pay attention to which types of value offerings are most appreciated
   - Adjust your approach based on feedback and results

Overcoming Challenges in Offering Value

1. Time Constraints
   - Prioritize high-impact value offerings
   - Integrate value-giving into your regular professional activities
   - Use tools and templates to streamline the process of sharing value

2. Fear of Overstepping
   - Start with small, low-risk offerings
   - Ask permission before providing extensive help or advice
   - Be sensitive to professional boundaries

3. Lack of Confidence
   - Remember that even small contributions can be valuable
   - Focus on your unique strengths and experiences
   - Seek feedback to build confidence in your value offerings

4. Avoiding Burnout
   - Set realistic limits on your value-giving activities

- Learn to say no to requests that overextend you
- Ensure you're also receiving value from your network

5. Maintaining Authenticity
   - Only offer value in areas where you have genuine expertise or interest
   - Be honest about your limitations and don't oversell your capabilities

The Long-Term Impact of Value-Based Networking

1. Enhanced Professional Reputation
   - Become known as a go-to resource in your field
   - Build a positive reputation as a generous and knowledgeable professional

2. Expanded Opportunities
   - Access to new job opportunities, collaborations, or projects
   - Increased visibility within your industry

3. Stronger, More Diverse Network
   - Develop deeper, more meaningful professional relationships
   - Attract a diverse range of contacts drawn to your value offerings

4. Personal and Professional Growth
   - Learn from the reciprocal value offered by your network
   - Develop new skills and insights through your value-giving activities

5. Increased Influence
   - Gain respect and credibility within your professional community
   - Have a greater impact on industry conversations and trends

6. Job Satisfaction and Fulfillment
   - Experience the personal satisfaction of helping others
   - Find greater meaning and purpose in your professional life

Remember, offering value is not about keeping score or expecting immediate returns. It's about genuinely contributing to your professional community and building positive, mutually beneficial relationships. By consistently offering value, you not only enhance your network but also contribute to a more collaborative and supportive professional environment for everyone.

Chapter 7: What Else to Consider

As we conclude our exploration of effective networking within professional organizations, it's important to consider some additional aspects that can significantly impact your networking success. This chapter will cover various elements that go beyond basic networking strategies, helping you to create a more holistic and successful approach to professional relationship-building.

Going Beyond Basic Networking

1. Develop a Networking Mindset
   - View networking as an ongoing process, not just an event-driven activity
   - Cultivate curiosity about others and their work
   - Approach networking with a spirit of generosity and mutual benefit

2. Emotional Intelligence in Networking
   - Develop self-awareness about your networking strengths and weaknesses
   - Practice empathy to better understand and connect with others
   - Manage your emotions effectively in professional settings

3. Cultural Competence
   - Be aware of cultural differences in networking practices
   - Adapt your approach when networking in diverse or international contexts
   - Show respect for and interest in different cultural perspectives

4. Networking Ethics
   - Always maintain honesty and integrity in your networking activities
   - Respect confidentiality and professional boundaries
   - Avoid exploitative or manipulative networking practices

5. Balancing Online and Offline Networking
   - Leverage both digital platforms and in-person interactions

- Understand the strengths and limitations of each approach
- Create a cohesive networking strategy that integrates both online and offline elements

Finding Mentors and Becoming One

1. Seeking a Mentor
   - Identify potential mentors who align with your career goals
   - Approach potential mentors respectfully and clearly articulate what you hope to learn
   - Be prepared to offer value in return, even as a mentee

2. Making the Most of Mentorship
   - Set clear goals and expectations for the mentorship relationship
   - Be proactive in scheduling meetings and preparing discussion topics
   - Show appreciation for your mentor's time and insights

3. Transitioning to a Mentor Role
   - Recognize when you have valuable experience to share with others
   - Be open to mentoring opportunities within your organization or professional community
   - Develop your listening and coaching skills

4. Benefits of Being a Mentor
   - Gain new perspectives and insights from your mentees
   - Enhance your leadership and communication skills
   - Contribute to the growth of your profession and leave a lasting legacy

5. Creating a Mentorship Culture
   - Advocate for mentorship programs within your organizations
   - Share your mentorship experiences to encourage others to participate
   - Foster an environment of continuous learning and support

Advancing Your Career Through Networking

1. Strategic Career Planning
   - Use your network to gather insights about potential career paths
   - Identify skill gaps and seek opportunities to develop them through your network
   - Stay informed about industry trends and emerging opportunities

2. Building a Personal Advisory Board
   - Cultivate relationships with a diverse group of professionals who can offer different perspectives
   - Seek advice on major career decisions from your trusted network
   - Be willing to offer similar support to others in return

3. Leveraging Your Network for Job Search
   - Keep your network informed about your career goals and job search status
   - Seek informational interviews to learn about potential opportunities
   - Use your network for recommendations and referrals

4. Developing Leadership Skills
   - Take on leadership roles within professional organizations
   - Seek feedback on your leadership style from your network
   - Use your network to learn about different leadership approaches and best practices

5. Building a Personal Brand
   - Consistently communicate your professional identity across all networking channels
   - Seek opportunities to showcase your expertise through your network
   - Cultivate a reputation for reliability and value within your professional community

Overcoming Common Networking Challenges

1. Dealing with Rejection
   - Understand that not every networking attempt will be successful
   - Learn from unsuccessful interactions and adjust your approach
   - Maintain a positive attitude and persistence in your networking efforts

2. Managing Network Size and Quality
   - Focus on building meaningful connections rather than accumulating contacts
   - Regularly assess and prune your network to maintain its relevance and value
   - Invest more time in high-potential relationships

3. Staying Motivated in Long-term Networking
   - Set specific networking goals and track your progress
   - Celebrate small wins and milestones in your networking journey
   - Remind yourself of the long-term benefits of consistent networking

4. Balancing Networking with Other Professional Responsibilities
   - Integrate networking into your daily work routine
   - Use time management techniques to allocate time for networking activities
   - Look for networking opportunities within your existing professional tasks

5. Overcoming Networking Anxiety
   - Start with small, manageable networking goals to build confidence
   - Prepare talking points or questions in advance of networking events
   - Practice self-care and relaxation techniques to manage anxiety

Emerging Trends in Professional Networking

1. Virtual and Hybrid Networking
   - Adapt to the increasing prevalence of online and hybrid networking events
   - Develop skills for effective virtual relationship-building
   - Stay informed about new digital networking platforms and tools

2. AI and Networking
   - Explore how AI can enhance your networking efforts (e.g., relationship management tools, networking suggestions)
   - Be aware of the ethical considerations surrounding AI in professional networking

3. Sustainability and Social Responsibility in Networking
   - Consider the environmental impact of your networking activities
   - Look for opportunities to align your networking with social responsibility goals

4. Cross-industry Networking
   - Explore networking opportunities beyond your immediate industry
   - Seek diverse perspectives and innovative ideas through interdisciplinary connections

5. Personal Data and Privacy in Networking
   - Be mindful of data privacy concerns in your networking activities
   - Understand and respect others' preferences for data sharing and communication

The Ongoing Journey of Professional Networking

Remember that effective networking is an ongoing process that evolves throughout your career. It requires consistent effort, adaptability, and a genuine interest in building mutually beneficial relationships. By incorporating the strategies and considerations discussed in this book, you can create a robust and dynamic professional network that supports your career growth, provides valuable opportunities, and contributes to your overall professional satisfaction.

As you continue on your networking journey, stay open to new approaches, be willing to learn from both successes and setbacks, and always strive to offer value to your professional community. With patience, persistence, and a strategic approach, you can build a network that not only advances your career but also enriches your professional life in meaningful ways.

Conclusion

Effective networking within professional organizations is a powerful tool for career advancement, personal growth, and mutual support among professionals. Throughout this book, we've explored various aspects of networking, from joining the right organizations to building lasting relationships and offering value to your professional community.

Key takeaways include:

1. Be selective in choosing professional organizations that align with your career goals and offer meaningful opportunities for engagement.

2. Actively participate in your chosen organizations, contributing your time, skills, and insights to become a valued member.

3. Focus on building genuine, lasting relationships rather than merely collecting contacts.

4. Follow up consistently and thoughtfully to nurture your professional connections.

5. Maintain visibility within your network through regular engagement and by sharing your expertise.

6. Consistently offer value to your network, creating a culture of mutual support and reciprocity.

7. Consider additional factors such as finding mentors, advancing your career through networking, and staying abreast of emerging trends in professional relationship-building.

Remember, effective networking is not a one-time event but an ongoing process that requires dedication, authenticity, and a genuine interest in others. By applying the strategies and insights shared in this book, you can develop a robust professional network that not only supports your career goals but also contributes to the growth and success of your entire professional community.

As you continue on your networking journey, remain open to new opportunities, be willing to adapt your approach, and always strive to add value to your professional relationships. With persistence and a strategic mindset, you can build a network that propels your career forward and enriches your professional life in meaningful ways.

Networking is both an art and a science. It requires practice, reflection, and continuous improvement. As you implement these strategies, you'll likely encounter challenges and celebrate successes. Embrace both as learning opportunities, and don't hesitate to adjust your approach as you grow and as your professional landscape evolves.

Finally, remember that at its core, networking is about human connections. While strategy and technique are important, genuine interest in others, empathy, and integrity are the foundations of truly successful networking. As you build your network, aim not just for professional success, but for the creation of a supportive, collaborative professional community that benefits all its members.

Your network is one of your most valuable professional assets. Nurture it wisely, and it will support you throughout your career journey.

References and Reading Suggestions

References:

1. Carnegie, D. (1936). How to Win Friends and Influence People. Simon & Schuster.

2. Coburn, D. (2014). Networking Is Not Working: Stop Collecting Business Cards and Start Making Meaningful Connections. BookBaby.

3. Sutton, R. I. (2007). The No Asshole Rule: Building a Civilized Workplace and Surviving One That Isn't. Business Plus.

4. Gerber, S., & Paugh, R. (2018). Superconnector: Stop Networking and Start Building Business Relationships that Matter. Da Capo Lifelong Books.

5. Ballinger, M., & Perez, N. A. (2016). The 20-Minute Networking Meeting. Career Innovations Press.

6. Ferrazzi, K., & Raz, T. (2005, updated 2014). Never Eat Alone: And Other Secrets to Success, One Relationship at a Time. Crown Business.

Further Reading Suggestions:

1. Misner, I., & Davis, R. (2017). Business Networking and Sex: Not What You Think. Entrepreneur Press.

2. Robinett, J. (2019). Crack the Funding Code: How Investors Think and What They Need to Hear to Fund Your Startup. AMACOM.

3. Kawasaki, G. (2015). The Art of the Start 2.0: The Time-Tested, Battle-Hardened Guide for Anyone Starting Anything. Portfolio.

4. Baber, A., & Waymon, L. (2007). Make Your Contacts Count: Networking Know-How for Business and Career Success. AMACOM.

5. Klauser, H. A. (2011). Write It Down, Make It Happen: Knowing What You Want And Getting It. Simon & Schuster.

6. Godin, S. (2008). Tribes: We Need You to Lead Us. Portfolio.

7. Gladwell, M. (2000). The Tipping Point: How Little Things Can Make a Big Difference. Little, Brown and Company.

8. Pink, D. H. (2012). To Sell Is Human: The Surprising Truth About Moving Others. Riverhead Books.

9. Grant, A. (2013). Give and Take: A Revolutionary Approach to Success. Viking.

10. Ury, W. (1991). Getting to Yes: Negotiating Agreement Without Giving In. Penguin Books.

These references and further reading suggestions cover various aspects of networking, relationship-building, and professional development, which can complement and expand upon the ideas presented in Dr. Jezek's ebook.

Links:
[1] https://www.linkedin.com/advice/1/heres-how-you-can-effectively-network-tnbae
[2] https://www.researchgate.net/publication/264351995_Understanding_the_role_of_networking_in_organizations
[3] https://timewellscheduled.com/how-to-use-professional-networking-effectively/
[4] https://ioufinancial.com/9-books-with-advice-to-make-networking-less-excruciating/
[5] https://careers.umbc.edu/students/network/networking101/tips/
[6] https://hbr.org/2016/05/learn-to-love-networking

[7]   https://www.cvsimply.com/blog/5-famous-books-about-professional-networking-you-should-not-miss

[8] https://www.researchgate.net/publication/240696871_Learning_The_Art_of_Networking_A_Critical_Skill_for_Enhancing_Social_Capital_and_Career_Success

[9]   https://www.indeed.com/career-advice/career-development/networking-strategies

.